**Andrews McMeel
Publishing**

Kansas City

This book is dedicated
to baristas everywhere,
especially those willing to fix
me a free espresso.

And a special acknowledgment to Jim Berry
of The Stage Right Cafe, Issaquah,Washington,
for his friendship, support,
and generosity (free espresso)
in helping to fuel (lots of free espresso)
my creativity.

—Brian Basset

Other Books by Brian Basset

Adam

Life in the Fast-Food Lane

Life Begins at 6:40

Minivanity

Bless This Home Office . . . with Tax Credits

WHAT'RE YOU STILL DOING HOME?

I DON'T GO INTO WORK UNTIL NOON THESE DAYS.

SINCE WHEN??

SINCE THREE WEEKS AGO, SILLY.

I REALLY NEED TO START BREWING STRONGER COFFEE.

SEE THIS GUY COMING IN... HOW MUCH YOU WANNA BET HE'S A MOCHA DRINKER?...WATCH.

A DOUBLE-TALL MOCHA, PLEASE.

THAT WAS EASY. HE'S A REGULAR, RIGHT?

NOPE.

CHOCOLATE DEPOSITS IN THE CORNERS OF HIS MOUTH LEFT BY THE REMNANTS OF PREVIOUS MOCHAS.

LOOK, THIS IS ONLY A PART-TIME JOB FOR ME, *NOT A CAREER.*

SO, BRYN. DO YOU LIKE BEING A BARISTA?

ONLY JOB I'VE EVER WANTED.

OH, C'MON. I FIND THAT HARD TO BELIEVE.

IT'S TRUE. EVER SINCE I WAS A LITTLE BOY AND HAD TO WATCH MY MOTHER DRINK VENDING MACHINE COFFEE.

THAT'S AWFUL! I HEARD STORIES LIKE THAT WHEN I WAS LITTLE BUT THOUGHT THEY WERE JUST MADE UP BY GROWN-UPS TO SCARE US KIDS.

WELL, MY MOTHER IS BARELY-LIVING PROOF OF IT.

BARISTA! THERE'S A CHOCOLATE SWIRL IN MY MOCHA! IF I HAD WANTED A CHOCOLATE SWIRL I WOULD'VE ASKED FOR ONE!

HERE, LET ME FIX YOU A NEW DRINK.

BRYN, WHAT'RE YOU DOING? HE SAID HE DIDN'T WANT ANY SWIRLS IN HIS MOCHA.

RIGHT, AND HE'S OBVIOUSLY A WARPED AND BITTER PERSON WHO FEELS COMPLETELY UNLOVED—SO I PUT A HEART DESIGN IN IT THIS TIME.

BRIAN BASSET

HI, THIS IS ADAM NEWMAN. I'M DOING YOUR COMPANY NEWSLETTER AND I HAVE ONE QUICK QUESTION.

BRIAN BASSET

I HAVE THE PHOTOS OF LAST MONTH'S COMPANY PICNIC UP ON MY SCREEN. DO YOU WANT ME TO TAKE OUT THE KETCHUP AND MUSTARD STAINS THAT'RE ALL OVER YOUR PRESIDENT'S SHIRT AND FACE?

SURE. I CAN ADD MORE.

I LIKE TO START MY DAY OFF RIGHT WITH A PIPING HOT PLATE OF FROZEN WAFFLES!

I ALWAYS THOUGHT YOU LIKED TO START YOUR DAY WITH A PIPING HOT BOWL OF OATMEAL?

I DID.

BRIAN BASSET

BUT THE WAFFLE PEOPLE ARE SHOWING MUCH BETTER COMMERCIALS RIGHT NOW.

GRRRRRRRRRR

NOW WHAT'S WRONG?

THE COMPUTER. IT'S ACTING UP AGAIN.

YO! FAT FINGERS! I'M SO FAST, YOU'RE SO SLOW. HEY, HUMAN, CAN YOU DO THIS?

NAH-NAH-NAH-NAH-NAH YOU CALL THIS A HOME OFFICE?! PPPHHHT!

HEY, MR. NEWMAN. YOU SURE HAVE BEEN IN HERE A LOT LATELY.

YEAH, I KNOW. SOMETIMES I THINK I'D SAVE A WHOLE BUNCH OF TIME AND MONEY IF I JUST BOUGHT MY OWN COPIER.

WHAT STOPS YOU?

THE LITTLE BOWL OF CANDIES YOU KEEP OUT BY THE REGISTER.

GUESS I SHOULD GET BACK TO THE COMPUTER AND BE PRODUCTIVE.

BRIAN BASSET

ADAM. COME INTO TOWN, ADAM.... COFFEE... ESPRESSO.... DOUBLE-TALL MOCHA...... MAYBE YOU'LL BE ABLE TO GET IN A WORKOUT AT THE GYM AFTERWARD.... COME INTO TOWN, ADAM. COME INTO TOWN.

IF IT ISN'T OUR OWN JOAN OF ARC ON A CRUSADE FOR CAFFEINE.

I HEARD VOICES.

Adam @home

BY BRIAN BASSET

HERE THEY COME.

TRIPLE MOCHA WITH TWO EXTRA SHOTS.

SINGLE SHORT LATTE.

DOUBLE-TALL SKINNY VANILLA.

GRANDE HAZELNUT WITH WHOLE MILK.

EVER NOTICE HOW PEOPLE RESEMBLE THEIR DRINKS?.. SOME MORE THAN OTHERS.

TALL AMERICANO!

BRIAN BASSET

11

SORRY I'M LATE, HAD TO DROP MY LITTLE GUY OFF AT NEIGHBORS. WHERE'S RUBY?

ON ASSIGNMENT, I'M HER HUSBAND, BERNARD. PLEASED TO MEET YOU.

THAT'S RIGHT, YOU'RE BOTH TRAVEL WRITERS WHO ARE NEVER HOME AT THE SAME TIME. I SEE YOU JUST GOT BACK FROM AFRICA OR INDIA.

NO.

BLOOMINGTON, MINNESOTA. THE MALL OF AMERICA.

BRIAN BASSET

EXCUSE ME, DO YOU CARRY BOOKS ON TAPE?

AGAINST THAT WALL OVER THERE.

OH GOOD, I'M GOING ON A LONG CAR TRIP WITH THREE KIDS AND A DOG. IS THERE ANYTHING YOU SUGGEST?

YES. FLY.

BRIAN BASSET

RINNNG

MISTLETOE ENTERPRISE. HOW MAY I DIRECT YOUR CALL?

ONE MOMENT PLEASE WHILE I TRANSFER YOU TO OUR COMPLAINT DEPARTMENT.

BRIAN BASSET

I NEVER GET TO STAY UP LATE!

MY ALLOWANCE IS TOO SMALL!!

SCHOOL STARTS TOO EARLY!

THEY HARDLY EVER FIX ANYTHING I LIKE TO EAT!

MY SISTER BUGS ME!

Adam @home

By Brian Basset

13

Adam @home

BY BRIAN BASSET

WUMP!

SOMETHING'S WRONG WITH MY COMPUTER.

REPAIRS

IT'S AS IF IT'S CURSED.

"CURSED."

Y'KNOW, LIKE THE SYSTEM'S BEEN CORRUPTED OR SOMETHING. MAYBE IT'S A VIRUS.

"CORRUPTED".... "VIRUS."

SCRIBBLE SCRIBBLE SCRIBBLE

OKAY, SIR. I'LL HAVE OUR RESIDENT EXPERTS TAKE A LOOK AT IT. GIVE US A FEW DAYS.

BRIAN BASSET

TECH SERVICES

VOTE ME EARLY & OFTEN

I PICKED US UP A MOVIE FOR TONIGHT.

WAIT! THIS IS A "CHICK FLICK."

NO....

I BELIEVE THERE'S A FLASHBACK SCENE SOMEWHERE TOWARD THE MIDDLE WITH WORLD WAR II AIRCRAFT IN IT.

OH, GOOD! I'LL MAKE SOME POPCORN!

BRIAN BASSET

UM, YES, MA'AM. YOUR ORDER IS BEING PROCESSED AND SHOULD BE READY FOR PRINTING AND SHIPPING ON...

UM, CAN YOU HANG ON A SEC? THANKS.

NOV

...EITHER THE DAY AFTER THE GUY COMES TO PRESSURE-WASH OUR HOUSE, OR THE DAY BEFORE I GO ON A FIELD TRIP WITH MY DAUGHTER'S CLASS.

BRIAN BASSET

KNOCK KNOCK

STACY CAME OVER TO PLAY WITH ME, SO DON'T BUG US!

TWO AGAINST ONE. *THAT* WOULD MAKE *ME* THE VICTIM.

BRIAN BASSET

Adam @ home

BY BRIAN BASSET

2:17

ADAM WAKE UP!

HUH? WHAT? DID I SAY SOMETHING IN MY SLEEP I PROBABLY SHOULDN'T HAVE??

WITH SKYROCKETING TUITION COSTS, HOW WILL WE EVER AFFORD TO SEND THREE KIDS TO COLLEGE?!?

I WOULDN'T WORRY ABOUT IT TOO MUCH. ONE OF THEIR BEANIE BABIES WILL BE WORTH MILLIONS BY THEN.

BRIAN BASSET

17

ADAM, DEAR... IF YOUR COMPUTER AND PRINTER AND FAX MACHINE ARE IN THE LAUNDRY ROOM...

... HOW COME I'M ALWAYS FINDING PRINTOUTS AND NOTES AND PHONE NUMBERS AND DISKS AND EMPTY CARTRIDGES AROUND THE HOUSE?!

BRIAN BASSET

IT *IS* A HOME OFFICE.

MOTHER, WHERE'S FATHER? ...AND WHEN WILL HE BE COMING HOME?

HE'S OFF ON SOME TRAVEL JUNKET IN THE SOUTH PACIFIC!...AND WHEN WE'LL SEE HIM SOON IS ANYONE'S GUESS. YOUR FATHER IS QUITE THE FREE SPIRIT, Y'KNOW.

YES, I DO. THAT MUST BE WHERE I GET IT FROM!...FATHER BEING A PRODUCT OF THE 1960s AND ALL.

BRIAN BASSET

WHAT ABOUT ME??

OH, MOTHER— PA-LEEEEEEASE! YOU DIDN'T GRADUATE FROM HIGH SCHOOL UNTIL THE EARLY '70s!

MOTHER, I'M GOING OUT.

LOOKING LIKE THAT?? I DON'T THINK SO, ARUBA.

OH, MOTHER! AND WHAT'S WRONG WITH THE WAY I LOOK?!

SEE FOR YOURSELF IN A MIRROR AND THEN YOU TELL ME.

THANK YOU, MOTHER! I DIDN'T HAVE MY NAVEL RING IN!

YOU'RE WELCOME, DEAR.

BRIAN BASSET

18

19

DAD, CAN YOU HELP ME WITH MY SCIENCE FAIR PROJECT?

SURE!

THANKS! I'M MAKING A VOLCANO THAT SPEWS OUT LAVA.

AND YOU NEED ME TO HELP YOU WITH THE PAPIER-MÂCHÉ?

NO, I NEED YOU TO BE THE HUMAN SACRIFICE TO THE GODS.

THERE! ALL DONE. I GUARANTEE THAT MY VOLCANO WILL BE THE TALK OF THE SCIENCE FAIR TOMORROW NIGHT!

WHAT IF IT DOESN'T ERUPT TOMORROW NIGHT WHEN ALL THE PARENTS ARE AT THE SCIENCE FAIR?

IT'S NOT SUPPOSED TO ERUPT AT THE SCIENCE FAIR.

I'VE DESIGNED IT SO IT'LL START SPEWING OUT LAVA ABOUT AN HOUR AFTER DAD DRIVES ME TO SCHOOL WITH IT IN THE MORNING.

... AND BY LUNCHTIME, THEY'LL BE SENDING US ALL HOME.

CAN IT BE SOONER? I HAVE A SPELLING TEST AFTER FIRST RECESS.

CLAYTON, WE ARE VERY PROUD OF THE EFFORT YOU PUT INTO YOUR SCIENCE FAIR PROJECT.

YES, YOU DID A TERRIFIC JOB.

MAPLE HILLS SCIENCE FAIR

BUT IT DIDN'T ERUPT.

IT WAS SUPPOSED TO COVER THE ENTIRE SCHOOL IN A THICK GOOEY LAVA.

AND THAT'S SOMETHING YOU ACTUALLY WANTED TO HAPPEN?

WELL, YEAH! THE LAVA'S MADE OF CHOCOLATE SYRUP!

BRIAN BASSET

Panel 1: OKAY. IT SAYS THAT BEN'S DOG, BUSTER, HAD A LITTER OF SIX PUPPIES.

Panel 2: IF BEN SOLD EACH PUPPY FOR $50, YET HIS EXPENSES IN CARING FOR THEM CAME TO $100, HOW MUCH PROFIT DID BEN MAKE FROM THEIR SALE?

BRIAN BASSET

Panel 3: SCRIBBLE SCRIBBLE SCRIBBLE SCRIBBLE SCRIBBLE SCRIBBLE SCRIBBLE SCRIBBLE SCRIBBLE

Panel 4: WHAT'S THIS??

A DRAWING OF SIX PUPPIES HOWLING AS THEY'RE BEING TORN FROM THEIR MAMA.

Panel 5: SORRY I'M LATE, GANG. MY 15-YEAR-OLD SON MISSED THE BUS AND HAD TO BE DRIVEN TO SCHOOL.

NO PROB.

YEAH, IT'S NOT LIKE THIS IS A MANDATORY MEETING.

Panel 6: I KNOW, BUT I LOOK FORWARD TO COMING HERE. EVEN THOUGH I SEE PATIENTS NEARLY EVERY DAY, WORKING FROM HOME OFTEN SEEMS LIKE...

A LONG LONELY VOYAGE ACROSS AN OPEN OCEAN VOID OF ANY STIMULATING ADULT CONTACT.

Panel 7: BRIAN BASSET

YES! YES! YES!

DID I SAY "CONTACT"? I MEANT "CONVERSATION."

GROUP HUG!

Panel 8: WHAT'S NEW WITH YOU, RUBY?

NOT MUCH. I JUST FINISHED A FREE-LANCE PIECE. PAID OKAY.

Panel 9: OH, AND BERNARD'S OFF ON SOME TRAVEL JUNKET IN THE CARIBBEAN.

WHY DIDN'T YOU GO WITH HIM?

Panel 10: HEAVENS NO! LET SOME OTHER WOMAN PICK UP AFTER HIM FOR A WHILE.

BRIAN BASSET

Panel 11: BERNARD HAS A MISTRESS??

NO. I'M TALKING ABOUT THE MAID AT HIS HOTEL.

Adam @ home
By Brian Basset

IT SURE WAS NICE SEEING PETER AND DEBBIE AGAIN.

PETER AND DEBBIE? DIDN'T WE JUST HAVE DINNER WITH MIKE AND CAROL?

WE NEED TO GET OUT MORE.

SORRY WE'RE LATE. EVERYTHING GO OKAY?

YUP.

ALTHOUGH CLAYTON DIDN'T EXACTLY GO TO BED WITHOUT A PROTEST.

SO HOW MUCH DO WE OWE YOU FOR TONIGHT?

$14,525

BRIAN BASSET

I KNOW WE WERE OUT LATER THAN WE SAID, BUT ISN'T BABY-SITTING JUST A PART-TIME JOB SO YOU CAN SAVE UP FOR COLLEGE?

YES. STANFORD OR HARVARD.

25

DING DONG.

THANKS.

I REALLY NEED TO START BRINGING A CAMERA ON MY ROUTE.

HMMMPH. I GUESS IT WAS JUST A MATTER OF TIME.

CLICK CLICK

WHAT'S THAT, ADAM?

OH, I WAS JUST READING THE NEWS ONLINE, AND Y'KNOW ALL THAT TROUBLE MICROSOFT HAD WITH THE JUSTICE DEPARTMENT?..

UN-HUH.

WELL, THEY JUST ACQUIRED THE JUSTICE DEPARTMENT.

KATY, WANNA SEE ME SHOOT A GRAPE OUT MY NOSE?!

NO! GO AWAY!

HERE GOES!...

NOMMM

WHAT'S THE POINT OF SHOOTING A GRAPE OUT YOUR NOSE IF NO ONE'S THERE TO SEE IT?

Adam @ h⊙me

by Brian Basset

DING
DONG

ZOOOM

WHAT AN EFFICIENT COMPANY. THEY DON'T STICK AROUND ONE SECOND LONGER THAN THEY HAVE TO.

MOTHER, GUESS WHAT?!

YOU BROKE UP WITH THAT BOY WHO NEVER SHOWERS?

NO, I GOT A JOB.

ARUBA, THAT'S GREAT! WHERE?!

AT YOUR FAVORITE ESPRESSO PLACE. THE ONE WHERE YOU HANG OUT WITH YOUR BUDDIES, ADAM AND TRUMAN.

MOTHER?? ARE YOU OKAY WITH THAT?

A BARISTA IN THE FAMILY!!... OH, ARUBA, YOU'VE MADE ME SOOOOO (SNIFF) HAPPY.

WHAT'S UP, RUBY?? YOU LOOK LIKE THE CAT WHO SWALLOWED THE CANARY.

YEAH, FILL US IN!

YOU'LL SEE.

HERE, GENTLEMEN, ON THE HOUSE!

?
?

MY DAUGHTER, ARUBA, JUST GOT A JOB HERE AT...

NO WONDER IT'S ON THE HOUSE... THIS IS THE WORST LATTE I'VE EVER HAD! THAT BARISTA SHOULD BE FIRED!

MY MOCHA IS LUKEWARM ... AND THIS ISN'T NON-FAT MILK.

Adam @ home

BY BRIAN BASSET

LAURA, YOU'RE GONNA BE LATE FOR WORK.

I KNOW I KNOW.

IT AMAZES ME HOW LONG IT TAKES YOU TO GET READY.

SORRY. WE CAN'T ALL WORK FROM HOME.

WHAT'RE YOU TALKING ABOUT? I'M NOWHERE NEAR READY FOR WORK. I HAVEN'T HAD MY SECOND CUP OF COFFEE YET.

G'MORNING, MR. NEWMAN. I HAVE A PACKAGE FOR YOU.

ON BEHALF OF THE THOUSANDS OF MEN AND WOMEN WHO WEAR THE PURPLE AND ORANGE, I WISH TO CONGRATULATE YOU ON BEING ONE OF OUR MOST LOYAL AND VALUED CUSTOMERS.

FOR ME?? THANKS!

HOW NICE. MORE ENVELOPES.

NICE WORK, TYLER.

TEACHER! OH TEACHER! THERE MUST BE SOME MISTAKE. IT SAYS D+ ON MY FOLDER!

THE ONLY MISTAKE WAS YOURS, CLAYTON. THE ASSIGNMENT WAS TO DO A REPORT ON A TROPICAL COUNTRY. YOU DID YOUR REPORT ON A TROPICAL FRUIT.

LAST TIME I CHECKED, THERE WAS NO COUNTRY NAMED MANGO.

WELL, THERE OUGHTTA BE. I THINK THE REPUBLIC OF MANGO SOUNDS PRETTY COOL.

33

JEANS AND A T-SHIRT?? THAT'S HOW YOU'RE GOING TO WORK?

IT'S CASUAL FRIDAY. WHAT'S WRONG?

NOTHING, IF YOU DON'T MIND LOOKING LIKE A SLOB.

BRIAN BASSET

THERE! MUCH BETTER.

EXCUSE ME, MISS. BUT IS **THIS** THE CORRECT PRICE ON THIS BOOK?? IT SEEMS SO HIGH FOR SUCH A TINY ITEM.

BACK WHEN I WAS A LITTLE GIRL WE USED TO GET BOOKS LIKE THIS <u>FREE</u> IN A BOX OF CRACKER JACK.

THAT'S ONE OF THOSE MINI BOOKS THAT ARE POPULAR THESE DAYS, AND YES, THAT'S THE ACTUAL PRICE.

WOULD YOU THROW IN A FREE BOX OF CRACKER JACK WITH IT?

BRIAN BASSET

EXCUSE ME, MISS. WHERE WOULD I FIND BOOKS ON THE BATTLE OF THE BULGE?

SECOND TO THE LAST ROW, IN MILITARY **HISTORY**.

PARDON MY ASKING— BUT WERE YOU......

BRIAN BASSET

IN THE BATTLE? YES. YES, I WAS.

TOO BAD MY HUSBAND'S NOT HERE. HE'D LOVE TO MEET YOU. HE READS ANY-THING HE CAN ON THAT STUFF.

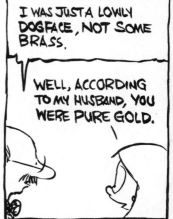

I WAS JUST A LOWLY DOGFACE, NOT SOME BRASS.

WELL, ACCORDING TO MY HUSBAND, YOU WERE PURE GOLD.

36

GOOD MORNING. WHAT TIME WERE YOU FINALLY ABLE TO FALL ASLEEP?

I DUNNO. IT WAS A WHILE AFTER I TALKED TO YOU, I KNOW THAT.

SO YOU DIDN'T TAKE MY ADVICE AND COUNT SHEEP?

NO, I DID.

BUT I MADE THEM CLONED SHEEP, ...AND IT TOOK TWICE AS LONG.

BRIAN BASSET

WHAT'RE YOU WATCHING?... ONE OF THOSE DISCOVERY CHANNEL PROGRAMS?

NO, IT'S THE TAPE OF YOU DELIVERING BABY NICK. IT WAS UP IN THE HALL CLOSET WITH THE OLD VIDEOS.

AND DO YOU EVER OWE US MONEY!! WE'VE HEARD TONS OF BAD WORDS COME OUT OF YOU.

HEY!

UP! UP!! WHERE'S THE REMOTE?!!

BRIAN BASSET

LAURA, CAN YOU COME HERE FOR A MOMENT?

BRIAN BASSET

SEE IF YOU CAN FIGURE OUT THIS MATH PROBLEM OF CLAYTON'S. I SURE CAN'T.

I'M CONVINCED THEIR CURRICULUM IS TEN TIMES MORE DIFFICULT THAN WHEN WE WERE KIDS.

SORRY. IT'S GREEK TO ME.

NO, HE FINISHED HIS GREEK AND LATIN EARLIER.

YES, YES. I CAN HAVE THAT DONE FOR YOU BY THAT DATE!

REALY. IT'S NO PROBLEM!

HELLO? HELLO??

CLICK

CLICK

NICK. YOU JUST HUNG UP ON A VERY IMPORTANT CALL.

AWWW, HECK. I NEVER WOULD'VE HAD IT DONE ON TIME.

I'M STARVED, DAD. WHAT'S FOR DINNER?!

SOMETHING I'M SURE YOU WON'T EAT.

BROCCOLI AND MEAT LOAF.

NO, I'LL EAT IT.

I MIGHT NOT DIGEST IT, BUT I'LL EAT IT.

WELL, GUYS. I'D BETTER HIT THE ROAD.

GOT WORK TO DO, RUBY?

HEAVENS NO.

GOT THREE MORE ESPRESSO PLACES DEPENDENT ON MY BUSINESS.

41

OOOW DAAAA MMMM DAH DAH DAHDY...

HE'S... AWAKE!

YES!! AND IF I HURRY I JUST MIGHT MAKE THAT OVERNIGHT DELIVERY DROP-OFF DEADLINE AFTER ALL!

THANK YOU! THANK YOU! THANK YOU!

CLASS, TODAY WE'LL HEAR ABOUT THE EXCITING WORLD OF LAW ENFORCEMENT FROM CAPTAIN KIMERER, JAMIE KIMERER'S DAD!...

AND HIS POLICE DOG, REX.

WOOF WOOF

RUFF RUFF RUFF

BOW WOW.

BRIAN BASSET

ONE QUESTION AT A TIME, PLEASE.

HERE TO TALK ABOUT WHAT IT'S LIKE TO BE AN ARCHITECT WHO GETS TO DESIGN GREAT STRUCTURES IS OUR OWN ISAAC AXELROD'S FATHER, MR. KALMAN AXELROD.

HI, CLASS!

DAD, DOES BEING AN ARCHITECT PAY WELL?!?

(HEH-HEH) THAT ALL DEPENDS ON THE SCOPE OF THE PROJECT, BUT YES, ISAAC, IT CAN PAY VERY WELL.

BRIAN BASSET

THEN WHY IS MY ALLOWANCE SO SMALL?!

44

MOM, I'M OUT OF CLEAN SOCKS!

I HAVEN'T DONE A WASH. WEAR A PAIR OF KATY'S.

KATY'S ??

WHAT TEAM WEARS PINK AND YELLOW SOCKS WITH TINY HEARTS ALL OVER THEM?

JUST HIKE THE BALL!

BRIAN BASSET

KATY, WE NEED AN EXTRA BODY FOR FOOTBALL.

AND YOU WANT ME?!?

BRIAN BASSET

DAD, I THINK BABY NICK NEEDS HIS DIAPER CHANGED.

COULD YOU? I'M ON THE PHONE.

ME?? CHANGE NICK'S DIAPER?!

I'LL GIVE YOU A DOLLAR IF YOU DO.

BRIAN BASSET

KATY, 50 CENTS IF YOU CHANGE NICK'S DIAPER.

Adam @home

BY BRIAN BASSET

MY GOODNESS, LAURA!..WHAT ON EARTH DID YOU EVER DO TO TICK OFF MOTHER NATURE SO MUCH??

I DECIDED TO BE KIND TO THE ENVIRONMENT AND TAKE THE BUS TO WORK.

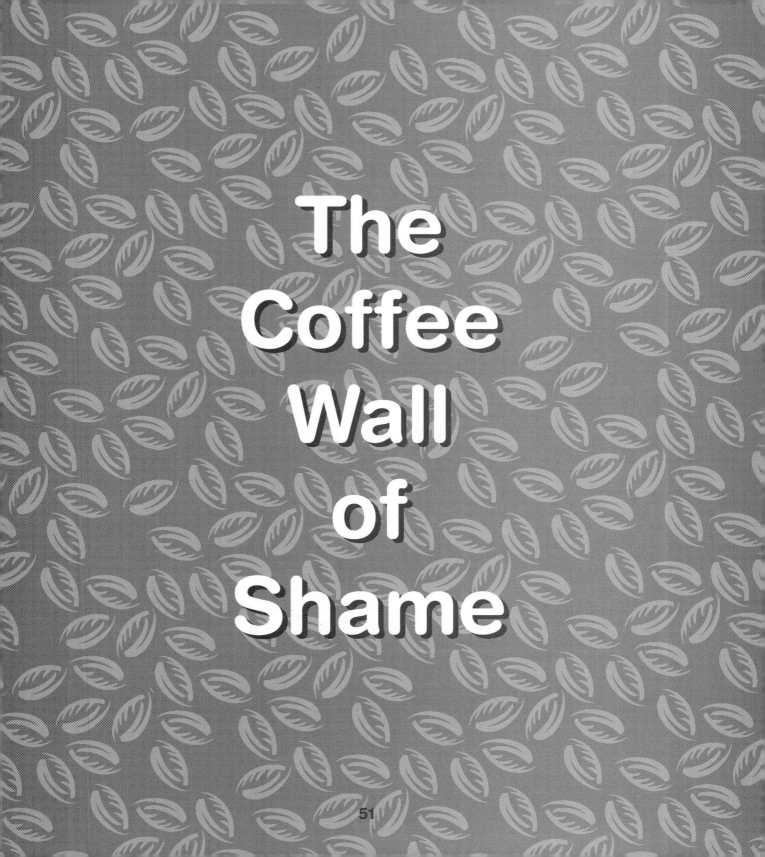

The Coffee Wall of Shame

DADDY! CLAYTON WON'T LEAVE ME AND EMILY ALONE!

HE KEEPS BOMBARDING US WITH SUBATOMIC PARTICLES FROM THE SUBATOMIC PARTICLE PULVERIZER HE CONSTRUCTED OUT OF EMPTY TOILET PAPER ROLLS!

DO I REALLY WANT TO STIFLE SUCH IMAGINATION AND CREATIVITY?

THIS ISN'T LIKE ADAM TO BE SO LATE.

I HOPE NOTHING'S WRONG.

I COULDN'T HAVE BEEN DRIVING *THAT* ERRATICALLY, OFFICER. I HAVEN'T HAD MY 8 SHOTS OF ESPRESSO YET.

AS YOU KNOW, FRIDAY IS OUR "FAVORITE" PERSON'S LAST DAY. DOES ANYONE WANT TO CHIP IN ON A GOING-AWAY GIFT?

EMPLOYEE BREAK RM.

NO ONE AROUND HERE REALLY LIKES HER.

I WAS THINKING ALONG THE LINES OF SOMETHING CHEESY AND TACTLESS.

OH, COUNT ME IN!

SAME HERE!

AWWW C'MON, LAURA. HELP ME WITH MY CHRISTMAS LETTERS!... IT'LL GIVE YOU MORE TIME WITH NICK!

I'M NOT QUITTING THE BOOKSTORE SO YOU CAN HAVE SOMEONE WATCH NICK FOR YOU. YOU SEEM TO FORGET WE NEED THE HEALTH INSURANCE IT PROVIDES.

HIRE A TEMP.

BRIAN BASSET

BUT WITH A TEMP I CAN'T WALTZ AROUND THE HOUSE IN MY BOXERS AND RATTY OLD T-SHIRTS.

SURE YOU CAN. YOU WANT TO DISCOURAGE ANY THOUGHTS OF AN OFFICE ROMANCE, DON'T YOU?

PAY UP, DAD. IT'S ALLOWANCE DAY!

DID YOU FINISH ALL YOUR CHORES?

WHAT DO YOU THINK I'VE BEEN DOING FOR THE PAST FOUR HOURS? I'VE BEEN UPSTAIRS CLEANING MY ROOM!

YOUR ROOM WAS MESSY, CLAYTON, BUT NOT THAT MESSY. IT SHOULD ONLY HAVE TAKEN YOU AN HOUR.

DOES THAT MEAN I GET PAID EXTRA FOR OVERTIME?!

WHAT'S THAT NOISE?!

WHAT NOISE?? I DIDN'T HEAR ANYTHING.

DOWNSTAIRS... IN THE KITCHEN. I'D BETTER INVESTIGATE. STAY HERE.

BRIAN BASSET

ADAM, DON'T YOU THINK YOU SHOULD TAKE A BASEBALL BAT WITH YOU?

CLICK

WHY? HOW'S A BASEBALL BAT GOING TO HELP ME EAT LEFTOVER PUMPKIN PIE??

Espresso Yourself

THE LAST SLICE OF PUMPKIN PIE RARELY GOES WITHOUT A FIGHT.

IT'S AMAZING HOW MANY PEOPLE I KNOW WHO WORK FROM HOME...

...DON'T WORK FROM HOME.

MUST BE NICE NOT HAVING TO GO INTO AN OFFICE EVERY DAY.

YES. YES IT IS.

TEACH ME. SHOW ME YOUR WAYS. LET ME BE YOUR PUPIL.

THE FIRST THING YOU SHOULD KNOW ABOUT WORKING FROM HOME IS THAT IT'S NOT ALL FUN AND GAMES.

YES!! I'VE FOUND THE SECRET PASSAGEWAY INTO THE DEATH CHAMBER!

SECONDLY: IT REQUIRES A TREMENDOUS AMOUNT OF SELF-DISCIPLINE.

ANOTHER MOCHA?

SURE! AND MAKE IT A TRIPLE!

PERSONALLY, I DON'T KNOW IF I HAVE WHAT IT TAKES TO WORK FROM HOME. I MEAN, YOU PRETTY MUCH HAVE TO GIVE UP YOUR OLD IDENTITY.

BRIAN BASSET

SOUNDS MORE LIKE THE WITNESS RELOCATION PROGRAM TO ME THAN A JOB.

WELL, THANKS FOR TAKING THE TIME TO TALK WITH ME, MR.... UM..., UM, I'M SORRY— I DIDN'T CATCH YOUR NAME.

SMITH. SMITH WILL DO JUST FINE.

DADDY, WHEN CAN WE GET OUR CHRISTMAS TREE?

YEAH! WHEN?!   HOW ABOUT...

...NOW?!

BRIAN BASSET

GIMME A SEC HERE WHILE I GRAB A COAT AND HAT AND THEN WE CAN GO.

GO WHERE??   YEAH— OUR SHOWS ARE ON!

KATY! TAKE A LOOK AT THIS TREE!

BRIAN BASSET

IT'S EXACTLY LIKE THE ONE FROM "A CHARLIE BROWN CHRISTMAS"!

HOW MUCH?? DAD SAID TO FIND AN INEXPENSIVE TREE.

$ 14,950 ?!!?

IT'S A COLLECTOR'S ITEM, KID!

Y'KNOW— THERE WERE A LOT MORE NEEDLES BEFORE YOU TOUCHED IT!

Ad@m

BY BRIAN BASSET

LISTEN!... UP ON THE ROOF!..... FOOTSTERS!

?

THEY'RE JUST SQUIRRELS.

AND WHAT ARE SQUIRRELS?...BUT TEENY-TINY REINDEER!

HOW DO YOU THINK A MAN AS BIG AS SANTA FITS DOWN A CHIMNEY?

BABY OIL. SOMETIMES HE USES HAND LOTION.

AND REINDEER. NOW DO THEY FLY??

IT'S NOT THE REINDEER. THEY JUST PULL THE SLEIGH FAST ENOUGH, KINDA LIKE AN ENGINE, TO CREATE "LIFT."

IT'S SANTA'S SLEIGH THAT ACTUALLY DOES THE FLYING. WE STUDIED "LIFT" AND "DRAG" LAST YEAR IN SCHOOL.

WELL, WHAT'S GOT ME IS HOW SANTA'S ABLE TO COVER THE ENTIRE GLOBE IN ONE NIGHT.

HE DOESN'T, REALLY. HALF THE WORLD DOESN'T CELEBRATE CHRISTMAS.

AHHHH, THE MYSTERY, MAGIC AND WONDERMENT THAT IS CHRISTMAS.

WHAT ABOUT BATHROOM BREAKS?

BRIAN BASSET

C'MON, ADAM, YOU CAN TELL ME. WHAT'RE YOU GIVING LAURA FOR CHRISTMAS?

DON'T LAUGH. UNDERWEAR.

WHAT'S TO LAUGH ABOUT? LOTS OF WOMEN ENJOY GETTING LINGERIE. ESPECIALLY SEXY LINGERIE.

TRUST ME, UNDERWEAR. *NOT* LINGERIE. THERE ARE SOME THINGS I FEEL MEN SHOULD NOT BUY THEIR WIVES... AND SEXY LINGERIE IS ONE OF THEM.

BECAUSE YOU RUN THE RISK OF TAKING THE "SURPRISE" OUT OF IT?

NO, BECAUSE YOU RUN THE RISK OF SAYING SOMETHING REALLY STUPID LIKE "GEE, IT LOOKED GOOD ON THE MODEL IN THE CATALOG."

BRIAN BASSET

MY WIFE IS *REALLY* HARD TO SHOP FOR. ANY SUGGESTIONS?

WHAT DID YOU GET HER LAST YEAR?

VINYL SIDING.

Y'KNOW, A GIRLFRIEND OF MINE SAID THERE ACTUALLY WERE MEN LIKE YOU.

DARN RIGHT! WOOD JUST DOESN'T HOLD UP AS WELL!!

BRIAN BASSET

DING DONG

HAPPY HOLIDAYS, MR. NEWMAN!

WELL, IF IT ISN'T THE CREW FROM MY FAVORITE COFFEE HANGOUT! COME ON IN!!

HERE, THESE ARE FOR YOU.

YOU SHOULDN'T HAVE!

THEY KIND OF COOLED DOWN ON THE WAY OVER HERE.

YOU SHOULDN'T HAVE!!

BRIAN BASSET

ARE YOU IN A CHAT ROOM?

UH-HUH, I'M HAVING A VIRTUAL HOME-OFFICE CHRISTMAS PARTY WITH OTHER HOME-OFFICE WORKERS.

CLICK CLICK

CLICK CLICK CLICK

GEEEESH, ADAM. EVERYONE'S SPELLING IS ATROCIOUS.

YEAH...

BRIAN BASSET

TOO MUCH VIRTUAL EGGNOG.

CLICK CLICK C

SANTA CAME! SANTA CAME!

MERRY CHRISTMAS.

I DON'T DO "MERRY" UNTIL I'VE HAD MY COFFEE.

71

Adam @ home
BY BRIAN BASSET

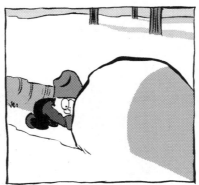

PAT
PAT

WHAT'CHA MAKING?

A SNOW ANGEL.

PAT
PAT
PAT

P
PAT
PAT
PAT
PA

IT WORRIES ME THAT I'M RELATED TO YOU.

BRIAN BASSET

IT'S AN ANAHEIM SNOW ANGEL

DAD, I FINISHED CLEANING MY ROOM!... AND I DID A REALLY, REALLY GOOD JOB, TOO!

JUST REMEMBER WHAT BEN FRANKLIN ONCE SAID, "WELL DONE IS BETTER THAN WELL SAID."

BRIAN BASSET

WELL SAID, DAD!

WAIT A SEC. NOW I'M REALLY CONFUSED.

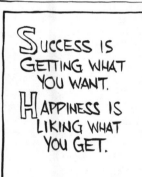

SUCCESS IS GETTING WHAT YOU WANT. HAPPINESS IS LIKING WHAT YOU GET.

BLESS THIS HOME OFFICE

WORK IN YOUR UNDIES TELECOMMUTE

BRIAN BASSET

EXERCISE OVER.

AW C'MON, YOU CALL THAT A WORKOUT?

BRIAN BASSET

MAYBE NOT FOR YOU...

Adam @ home

By Brian Basset

CLICK

GOOD FILM! OKAY, LET'S GO TO BED.

THE VIDEO HAS TO BE BACK BY MIDNIGHT, ADAM. WHO'S GONNA DRIVE IT IN — ME OR YOU?

LET'S JUST PAY THE LATE FEE.

NOOOO. LET'S DRIVE IT IN AND BE OVER WITH IT.

LAURA, I'M HAPPY PAYING THE LATE FEE. HONEST.

YOU OR ME, ADAM. WHO'S IT GONNA BE?

SERIOUSLY. I SAY WE GO TO BED NOW AND PAY THE LATE FEE IN THE MORNING.

WHERE ARE THE CAR KEYS?! I'LL GO!

OKAY, OKAY, GIVE ME THE VIDEO!!

I'LL JUST SIT OUT HERE FOR 10 MINUTES OR SO AND PAY THE LATE FEE IN THE MORNING. AFTER ALL, THERE IS THE PRINCIPLE OF THE THING!

BRIAN BASSET

DAD, WHERE'S THE VIDEO CAMERA?

UPSTAIRS IN THE HALL CLOSET. BUT I THINK THE BATTERY NEEDS TO BE RECHARGED.

YOU MEAN IT'S NOT READY TO GO??? WHAT IF ALIENS FROM A DISTANT STAR SYSTEM WERE TO SET FOOT ON OUR FRONT LAWN?!

I SUPPOSE THEY WOULDN'T BE VERY HAPPY..... CONSIDERING HOW THE NEIGHBORHOOD DOGS THINK OF IT AS THEIR OWN PRIVATE BATHROOM.

DAAAAAAAD! THAT'S NOT WHAT I MEANT!"

KATY, WANT TO BE IN MY NEW MOVIE I'M MAKING?!

NO. GO AWAY.

IT'S AN INTERGALACTIC SPACE VERSION OF THE 'WIZARD of OZ' AND YOU'D BE PERFECT FOR THE PART!

AS DOROTHY?!!

NO, AS THE WICKED DROID WHO GETS AN ASTEROID DROPPED ON HER.

PLACES, EVERYONE! LIGHTS... CAMERA...

ACTION!

UM... LENS CAP'S ON.

WELL, DUHHHHHHHH, THIS SCENE TAKES PLACE AT NIGHT.

BRIAN BASSET

REMEMBER, EVERYONE. THIS IS AN INTERGALACTIC VERSION OF "THE WIZARD OF OZ" SO IN THIS SCENE, DAD, YOU'RE TO JUMP OUT OF THE CARBON-DIOXIDE FOREST...

... AND LET OUT A REALLY FEROCIOUS ROAR AS DOROTHY AND HER GROUP WALK BY.

UM, LIKE THE COWARDLY LION?

I THINK TOTO NEEDS HIS DIAPER CHANGED.

MORE LIKE THE TIME YOU RAN INTO THE SPRINKLER BAREFOOT.

AND NO, KATY, WE CAN'T STOP SHOOTING. *THAT'S* JUST NOXIOUS GASES YOU SMELL.

MR. DIRECTOR! MR. DIRECTOR! I HAVE A QUESTION!

♪♪

MR. DIRECTOR, MR. PRODUCER, MR. CINEMATOGRAPHER, MR. SOUNDMAN, MR. WRITER, MR. KEY GRIP, MR. GAFFER, MR. SET DESIGNER AND MR. LIGHTING DIRECTOR I HAVE A QUESTION!

OKAY, KATY. IN THIS SCENE YOU (DOROTHY) MELT <u>MOM</u> (THE WICKED DROID OF THE WEST) BY DUMPING A PAIL OF ACID ON HER.

BUT SHE'S <u>OUR</u> MOM. I CAN'T MELT HER.

YES, SHE'S OUR MOM IN <u>REAL</u> LIFE, BUT <u>THIS</u> IS <u>REEL</u> LIFE!

MY POINT EXACTLY.

MOMMMMM! KATY'S RUINING MY BIG ACID-MELTING SCENE!!

SEE! EVEN YOU CALLED FOR **MOM**! ...<u>NOT</u> THE WICKED <u>DROID OF THE WEST</u>.

Ad@m

BY BRIAN BASSET

OH, NO!... THE POLICE!!

I CAN EXPLAIN EVERYTHING, OFFICER!

I WAS DRINKING A LATTE ON MY WAY BACK FROM THE STORE... I COULD BARELY HOLD IT IT WAS SO HOT... AND THEN I HIT A POTHOLE AND DROPPED IT ON MY LAP.

THAT'S WHY I WAS DRIVING SO ERRATICALLY, OFFICER.

WELL... AT THE VERY LEAST, I SHOULD CITE YOU FOR **NOT** HAVING AN INSULATED COMMUTER MUG WITH A SIP LATCH.

AS WELL AS DRIVING WITHOUT PROPER CUP HOLDERS.

BUT I WON'T.

INSTEAD, I'LL GET ON THE CITY TO FILL IN THAT DANGEROUS ROAD HAZARD.

THANK YOU, OFFICER.

I KNEW HE'D UNDERSTAND. AFTER ALL— COPS, DOUGHNUTS AND A CUP OF "JOE" ARE PART OF OUR CAFFEINE CULTURE.

AND DON'T FORGET TO ASK YOUR BARISTA TO FIX YOUR LATTES A FEW DEGREES COOLER, TOO!

THINK I'LL STOP FOR A BISCOTTI AND AN ESPRESSO ON MY WAY BACK TO THE STATION.

BRIAN BASSET

DAD, TOMORROW'S ST. PATRICK'S DAY. HOW 'BOUT IF I MISS SCHOOL AND GO TO THE BIG ST. PATRICK'S DAY PARADE DOWNTOWN INSTEAD ?!?

I DON'T THINK SO.

YOUR SCHOOLING IS MORE IMPORTANT.

HOW DO YOU FIGURE ?? I'M SURE TO FORGET WHATEVER'S TAUGHT IN CLASS TOMORROW, WHEREAS—I'LL PROBABLY REMEMBER THE PARADE FOR THE REST OF MY LIFE.

SEE— YOU MUST BE LEARNING SOMETHING... THAT'S PRETTY GOOD LOGIC.

HURRY DOWN YOU TWO OR YOU'LL BE LATE FOR SCHOOL!

GOOD GRIEF, CLAYTON! WHAT DID YOU DO TO YOUR HAIR ??!

I DYED IT GREEN FOR ST. PATRICK'S DAY.

DON'T WORRY, IT'S NOT PERMANENT. IT'LL GROW OUT.

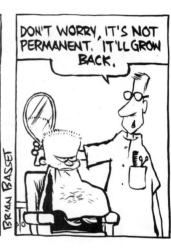

DON'T WORRY, IT'S NOT PERMANENT. IT'LL GROW BACK.

WHAT HAPPENED TO YOUR HAIR, CLAYTON ??

MY MOM HAD IT ALL CUT OFF BECAUSE I DYED IT GREEN FOR ST. PATRICK'S DAY AND THE DYE WOULDN'T COME OUT.

I THINK IT LOOKS COOL. KINDA MAKES YOU LOOK LIKE A ROCK STAR.

YOU THINK??

YEAH! ALL YOU NEED NOW IS AN EARRING... NO, BETTER YET— A NOSE RING!

HOW'S THIS LOOK ??

COOOOL!

BUS IS COMING.

Adam @ home
By Brian Basset

I'D LIKE A TALL LATTE. AND COULD YOU DOUBLE-CUP THAT, PLEASE?

ACTUALLY, COULD YOU TRIPLE-CUP IT? MY HANDS ARE RATHER SENSITIVE TO HEAT.

UM, NOW THAT I THINK ABOUT IT, YOU'D BETTER QUADRUPLE THAT. I'D HATE TO HAVE TO FILE A LAWSUIT AGAINST YOU GUYS IN CASE IT SOMEHOW SPILLED ON ME.

BETTER YET, 5-CUP IT JUST TO TO BE SAFE.

AHHH, WHAT THE HECK. ADD A FEW MORE WHILE YOU'RE AT IT... MORE... MORE...

SAY, ISN'T THAT THE GUY WHO RUNS THAT LITTLE ESPRESSO STAND DOWN THE STREET?

BRIAN BASSET

RING
RING
RING

CLICK CLICK CLICK CLICK

GOTCHA! I KNEW IF I TIMED IT JUST RIGHT AND THEN CALLED BACK, YOU'D BE PICKING UP THE PHONE TO CHECK MESSAGES!

NEWMAN, I'M FRUMPBACHER FROM THE NEIGHBORHOOD ASSOCIATION. IT'S ABOUT YOUR SIGN OUT BY YOUR DRIVEWAY.

YOU MEAN THE BIG "**QUALITY DESKTOP PUBLISHING AT REASONABLE PRICES**" SIGN?! YES!.... ADVERTISING REALLY DOES PAY!

SO WHAT CAN I DO FOR YOU, FRUMPSTER?

WELL, UM, I, UM GUESS THE NEXT NEIGHBORHOOD ASSOCIATION NEWSLETTER WOULD BE NICE.

HEY!

YOU'RE BACK.

THAT I AM, NEWMAN. AND **THIS** TIME YOU WON'T GET RID OF ME SO EASILY!

AS PRESIDENT OF THE NEIGHBORHOOD ASSOCIATION I WANT TO POINT OUT HOW YOUR "QUALITY DESKTOP PUBLISHING" SIGN ERECTED ON YOUR PROPERTY IS IN DIRECT VIOLATION WITH COVENANTS PERTAINING TO "VISUAL LAWN DISPLAYS."

WHEN WERE THOSE COVENANTS ADOPTED?

UM, LEMME SEE ... AHHH, HERE IT IS. SEPTEMBER 1965, WHEN THE ASSOCIATION WAS FORMED. **WHY?**

FLIP FLIP

OH, NOTHING MUCH. JUST THAT PERSONAL COMPUTERS AND DESKTOP PUBLISHING DIDN'T EXIST BACK THEN.

OH ... RIGHT, RIGHT. FORGET IT THEN.

WHATCHA KEEP LOOKING AT OUT THAT WINDOW, RUTH?

THAT NICE YOUNG NEWMAN FELLOW FROM UP THE STREET.

EVERY MORNING HE SEES HIS CHILDREN OFF TO SCHOOL BY WALKING THEM DOWN TO THE BUS STOP IN FRONT OF OUR HOUSE.

WHAT A CARING, THOUGHTFUL...

HEY—HE'S READING *OUR* NEWSPAPER OUT OF *OUR* PAPER BOX WHILE WAITING FOR THE BUS!!

BRIAN BASSET

GEE, MR. NEWMAN, YOU DON'T SOUND YOUR NORMAL FRAZZLED SELF TODAY.

TOO TIRED I GUESS.

SO I DON'T SLIGHT THE KIDS DURING THE DAY I'M TRYING TO GET MY WORK DONE AT NIGHT.

I DON'T KNOW HOW YOU DO IT. WORKING FROM HOME MUST BE TOUGH.

Y'KNOW, YOU'RE THE FIRST PERSON TO ACKNOWLEDGE THAT!

...AND YOU'RE NOT EVEN A PERSON.

WELL, ONE DAY I HOPE TO BE INSIDE THE CLOWN COSTUME!

BRIAN BASSET

BRIAN BASSET

...SO I FINALLY HAD TO USE A COLLECTION AGENCY.

RING

I SEE...UH-HUH...UH-HUH... NO PROBLEM, LET ME CALL UP THAT RESERVATION AND SEE WHAT I CAN DO.

FLIP

MOBILE HOME OFFICE. RUBY'S BRIEFCASE IS LIKE A PORTABLE TRAILER PARK.

THERE'S A NON-STOP LEAVING PARIS AT....

PRRRRR

CLICK CLICK CLICK

I JUST GOT AN E-MAIL FROM ADAM. APPARENTLY HIS SON IS STILL NAPPING, SO HE SAYS HE'LL HAVE TO JOIN US IN CONVERSATION **THIS** WAY.

TELL HIM HE'S MISSING THE MOST PERFECT SHOTS OF ESPRESSO *EVER*! ...THAT THEY'VE *NEVER* BEEN FINER!

BRIAN BASSET

TYPE TYPE TYPE TYPE TYPE

HE SAYS... "MAY YOU FIND THE NOSE RING OF A BARISTA AT THE BOTTOM OF YOUR CUP."

ADAM SAYS NICK'S STILL NAPPING AND FOR US TO IMAGINE THAT THE TWO OF THEM ARE IN THEIR USUAL SPOTS AND THAT WE'RE HAVING A HEATED DISCUSSION ON NOTHING IN PARTICULAR.

TRUMAN! WHAT'RE YOU DOING?

BRIAN BASSET

ADAM *ALWAYS* SPILLS.

AND THEN THERE ARE THE MUFFIN CRUMBS AROUND HIS SEAT?...

AND!...AND!... *NOT* PUTTING THE NEWSPAPER BACK PROPERLY FOR THE NEXT PERSON?!...

ADAM SAYS NICK FINALLY WOKE UP FROM HIS NAP AND THE TWO OF THEM CAN BE HERE IN 15 MINUTES.

Y'KNOW, I'D LOVE TO STAY LONGER, BUT I HAVE A PATIENT TO SEE IN HALF AN HOUR.

THAT REMINDS ME. I'M GIVING A SPEECH THIS EVENING AT THE UNIVERSITY THAT I REALLY SHOULD PRACTICE FOR.

BRIAN BASSET

TYPE TYPE TYPE TYPE TYPE TYPE

AND **THEY** CALL THEMSELVES "COFFEE ADDICTS"?!

KID, SINCE YOU'RE NEW HERE AT KOPYKO, LET ME POINT OUT THE BIG DIFFERENCE BETWEEN US AND THOSE OTHER COPY CENTERS.

AT KOPYKO, WE BELIEVE THERE ARE NO IMPOSSIBLE REQUESTS.

YOU'VE GOTTA HELP ME!... YOU'VE GOTTA MAKE ME LOOK GOOD! I'VE GOT A BIG PRESENTATION IN LESS THAN AN HOUR, AND I NEED 1,000 COPIES COLLATED AND BOUND!

HOW 'BOUT A HAIRCUT AND A DIFFERENT TIE—ONE THAT'LL BRING OUT THE COLOR IN YOUR EYES?

THANKS! YOU GUYS ARE TERRIFIC!

HERE AT KOPYKO WE LIKE TO TREAT OUR VALUED CUSTOMERS LIKE EMPLOYEES.

DON'T YOU MEAN AS IF THEY WERE STOCKHOLDERS OF THE COMPANY?

FILL YOUR OWN MACHINE WITH PAPER, MRS. JOHNSON!

APPARENTLY NOT.

HERE AT KOPYKO, KID, WE'RE PROUD THAT MANY SMALL-BUSINESS PEOPLE AND HOME-OFFICE WORKERS MAKE OUR PLACE OF BUSINESS THEIR PLACE OF BUSINESS.

FOR EXAMPLE, SEE THAT WOMAN IN THE BLUE DRESS AT ONE OF THE WORK-STATIONS?

SHE'S IN HERE ALMOST EVERY DAY CONDUCTING BUSINESS FROM ONE OF THE MANY FREE PHONES WE ENCOURAGE OUR CUSTOMERS TO TAKE ADVANTAGE OF.

HELLO. DO YOU HAVE PRINCE ALBERT IN A CAN?..

85

AT KOPYKO, WE WANT OUR CUSTOMERS—ESPECIALLY THE SMALL-BUSINESS PERSON AND THE TELECOMMUTER—TO THINK OF US AS ANOTHER WAY TO "OFFICE!"

EVERYTHING'S HERE FOR THEM. A BANK OF FREE PHONES... WORKSTATIONS... COPIERS... COMPUTERS... PAPER CLIPS AND RUBBER BANDS.

BRIAN BASSET

STALE COFFEE. YOU HAVE THOUGHT OF EVERYTHING.

WE USE "VENDING MACHINE" BLEND TO GET THAT REAL OFFICE TASTE.

TELECOMMUTERS IN PARTICULAR SEEM TO ENJOY THE OFFICE ENVIRONMENT HERE AT KOPYKO OVER THEIR OWN PLACE.

ISN'T THAT RIGHT, MR. NEWMAN?!

I DUNNO. I THINK I GET BETTER RECEPTION AT HOME.

BATHROOM'S ALL YOURS.

HERE AT KOPYKO, KID, WE LIKE TO THINK OF OURSELVES AS THE OFFICE AWAY FROM THE OFFICE... ESPECIALLY FOR THE SMALL-BUSINESS PERSON AND TELECOMMUTER.

WE TRY TO PROVIDE ALL THE ESSENTIALS OF TODAY'S WORKPLACE... ONE THAT'S MODERN AND EFFICIENT— YET COMFORTABLY FAMILIAR.

BRIAN BASSET

WHY DOES HE ALWAYS GET THE GOOD COPIER MACHINE?? MINE EITHER NEEDS PAPER OR IS OUT OF TONER!

DON'T LISTEN TO HER! SHE ALWAYS GETS WHITE-OUT ON THE GLASS!!

IMPRESSIVE. YOU EVEN INCLUDED PETTY OFFICE POLITICS.

YUP.

Adam @home BY BRIAN BASSET

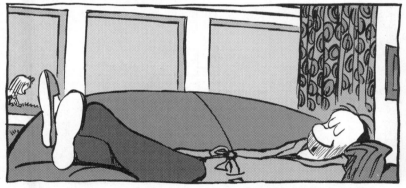

YOU'VE ELEVATED HIDING EASTER EGGS TO AN ART FORM, ADAM.

LEARNED IT FROM MY DAD. HE WAS THE MASTER.

87

Panel 1:
DADDY, TELEPHONE.

DID YOU ASK WHO WAS CALLING?

Panel 2:
UH-HUH. IT'S MY TEACHER.

UH-OH. YOU DIDN'T PUT PASTE IN THAT BOY'S HAIR AGAIN, DID YOU?

Panel 3:
OR SNIP SOME OF THAT REAL OBNOXIOUS GIRL'S HAIR LIKE LAST TIME??

NOTHING LIKE THAT! HONEST.

Panel 4:
I VOLUNTEERED YOU TO HELP IN OUR CLASS ROOM.

MR. NEWMAN, HI, GOOD EVENING. KATY MENTIONED TO ME TODAY HOW YOU'RE HOME DURING THE DAY.

BRIAN BASSET

Panel 5:
I REALLY APPRECIATE YOUR COMING IN TO HELP OUT IN THE CLASS ROOM TODAY.

HOWEVER I CAN BE OF HELP.

Panel 6:
THAT'S GREAT! WHAT SPECIAL SKILLS DO YOU HAVE?

WELL... EVEN THOUGH I WAS AN ENGLISH MAJOR, HISTORY AND SCIENCE HAVE ALWAYS BEEN MY FAVORITE SUBJECTS.

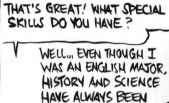

BRIAN BASSET

Panel 7:
NO, NO, NO...

Panel 8:
HAVE YOU OPERATED A LAMINATING MACHINE BEFORE?
HOW ARE YOU AT THUMBTACKING??
EVER CUT THROUGH TEN SHEETS OF CONSTRUCTION PAPER AT ONCE???
IMPORTANT STUFF LIKE THAT!

Panel 9:
OVER HERE IS WHERE I CAN REALLY USE YOUR HELP. I HAVE A FEW HUNDRED PAPERS THAT NEED TO BE GRADED, SORTED, AND PUT INTO EACH CHILD'S FOLDER.

BRIAN BASSET

Panel 10:
AFTER YOU'RE THROUGH WITH THAT, I NEED 350 OF EACH LETTER OF THE ALPHABET CUT OUT OF GREEN CONSTRUCTION PAPER AND THEN GLUE-STICKED TO A BLACK BACKGROUND THAT'S SLIGHTLY LARGER.

OUT OF CURIOSITY... DO YOU GET ANY OTHER PARENTS WHO VOLUNTEER?

Panel 11:
OHHH, A NUMBER OF THE MOMS COME IN A FEW DAYS A WEEK. THEY USUALLY HANG OUT IN THE SUPPLY ROOM WORKING ON PROJECTS.

Panel 12:
DON'T WORRY—YOU'LL GET TO MEET THEM... EVENTUALLY. NEW WORKERS AREN'T ALLOWED TO SPEAK TO THE OTHER VOLUNTEERS AT THE BEGINNING. TOO DISTRACTING.

I COULD TRY TO MAKE A BREAK FOR IT... BUT THERE ARE 29 STUDENTS WATCHING. Oooo

I GRADED AND THEN SORTED ALL OF THESE PAPERS ALPHABETICALLY LIKE YOU ASKED.

EXCELLENT.

I'M GOING TO GIVE YOU A GOLD STAR, MR. NEWMAN!

WERE YOU ABLE TO CUT OUT THE 350 LETTERS AND NUMERALS AND GLUE-STICK THEM TO THE STIFFER BOARD?

UM... I WAS JUST ABOUT TO START THAT...

TSK-TSK. I'LL JUST HAVE TO PUT THAT GOLD STAR BACK.

BRIAN BASSET

EXCELLENT JOB, MR. NEWMAN. I WANT TO THANK YOU FOR VOLUNTEERING YOUR TIME TODAY AND HELPING OUT IN OUR CLASSROOM.

ONE.... QUESTION.

RUMOR HAS IT YOU KEEP SOME OF YOUR STUDENTS BACK A GRADE IF THEIR PARENTS ARE PARTICULARLY HELPFUL IN THE CLASSROOM. IS THIS TRUE?

FLUNK MY STUDENTS JUST TO RETAIN GOOD PARENT-VOLUNTEERS?? HA-HA-HA- WHERE IN THE WORLD DID YOU HEAR THAT??

FROM ONE OF THE MOMS IN THE BACK ROW.

BRIAN BASSET

THAT'S NOT A MOM. THAT'S ONE OF MY STUDENTS!

ADAM, NICK'S FUSSING. IT'S YOUR TURN TO CHECK ON HIM. ADAM!

ADAM?!

BRIAN BASSET

AARRRGGGG! MEN CAN SLEEP THROUGH JUST ABOUT ANYTHING.

ESPECIALLY GUILT.

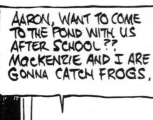

AARON, WANT TO COME TO THE POND WITH US AFTER SCHOOL?? MACKENZIE AND I ARE GONNA CATCH FROGS.

BUT WHATEVER YOU DO, DON'T TELL YOUR MOM HOW GROSS AND MESSY IT CAN BE. MOMS HATE THAT SORT OF THING.

HOW GROSS AND MESSY?

LAST WEEK AFTER I CAME HOME FROM THE POND... I FOUND A TADPOLE STUCK IN MY BELLY BUTTON.

I'M THERE!!

MACKENZIE, DON'T YOU JUST LOVE CATCHING FROGS?

YEAH, BUT WOULDN'T IT BE LESS OF A MESS IF WE KNELT BY THE SIDE OF THE POND INSTEAD OF WADING THROUGH ALL THIS?

SURE — IT WOULD BE CLEANER, BUT THAT'S NOT WHAT IT'S ALL ABOUT.

I MEAN, HOW MANY TIMES DOES A KID GET TO EXPERIENCE AN HONEST-TO-GOSH, REAL-LIFE LAUNDRY DETERGENT COMMERCIAL?!?

GOOD POINT, MAYBE ONLY 30 OR 40 IF HE'S LUCKY.

HOW DID YOUR FROG-CATCHING EXPEDITION GO?

GREAT, WE CAUGHT ABOUT 40 FROGS!

DON'T WORRY. I LET THEM ALL GO.

BACK IN THE POND OR IN KATY'S ROOM?!

92

Adam @home

By Brian Basset

WHAT'S TAKING SO LONG?!? I CAN'T BELIEVE IT'S TAKING SO LONG!!

I KNEW I SHOULD'VE HAD A CUP BEFORE LEAVING THE HOUSE!! WHY DIDN'T I HAVE A CUP BEFORE LEAVING THE HOUSE?!??

I'M NOT GOING TO MAKE IT. I'M NOT GOING TO MAKE IT. I'M NOT GOING TO MAKE IT. **I'M NOT GOING TO...**

BRIAN BASSET

P·O·O·F!

YES!! THE LINE'S MOVING.

WHOA, THAT COULD'VE BEEN ME.

Adam @ home

by Brian Basset

THUD!

BATTER, TAKE YOUR BASE.

NEXT BATTER!

BRIAN BASSET

STRETCHHHH

TRUDGE TRUDGE TRUDGE

MIND IF I USE **THAT** WHEN YOUR PITCHER IS THROWING?

KATY! CLAYTON! HURRY IT UP OR YOU'LL BE LATE FOR SCHOOL!

SILLY ME, I SPREAD PEANUT BUTTER ON BOTH PIECES OF BREAD.

OH, WELL, I'LL JUST PUT THE JELLY BETWEEN THE TWO LAYERS OF PEANUT BUTTER AND HOPE HE DOESN'T NOTICE.

MY SANDWICH. IT'S..... IT'S.....

WHERE'S THAT MUSIC COMING FROM?

...IT'S NOT SOGGY.

SOMETHING WRONG, CLAYTON?

IT'S MY PEANUT BUTTER AND JELLY SANDWICH. IT'S NOT SOGGY.

NOT SOGGY?? HOW CAN THAT BE?

I DUNNO. I SAW MY DAD IN THE KITCHEN THIS MORNING FIXING MY LUNCH LIKE HE ALWAYS DOES.

MAYBE HE USED A NEW KIND OF JELLY OR SOMETHING.

BUMMER. NOW YOU CAN'T ROLL IT UP INTO LITTLE BALLS AND THROW THEM AGAINST THE BUILDING AT RECESS.

I KNOW. A WASTE OF A PERFECTLY GOOD PB&J.

DAD, WE'RE HOME... AND HEY, GREAT PB&J TODAY!...IT WASN'T SOGGY AS USUAL. WHAT DID YOU DO DIFFERENT?

I'M NOT SURE, BUT IT MAY HAVE BEEN BECAUSE I GOT DISTRACTED THIS MORNING AND ENDED UP SPREADING THE PEANUT BUTTER ON BOTH PIECES OF BREAD.

SO I GUESS WHEN I PUT THE JELLY BETWEEN THE TWO LAYERS OF PEANUT BUTTER, IT ACTUALLY FORMED A SORT OF PROTECTIVE BARRIER.

DAD! YOU REINVENTED THE CLASSIC PEANUT BUTTER AND JELLY SANDWICH!

IS THERE ANY MONEY INVOLVED? I SURE HATE MAKING LUNCHES IN THE MORNING.

WHO YA WRITING TO?

ALL MY E-MAIL PALS!

CLICK CLICK CLICK CLICK CLICK

I'M TELLING THEM HOW OUR DAD REINVENTED THE PEANUT BUTTER AND JELLY SANDWICH BY PLACING THE JELLY BETWEEN TWO LAYERS OF PEANUT BUTTER INSTEAD OF DIRECTLY AGAINST THE BREAD.

CLICK CLICK CLICK

BRIAN BASSET

IN THE HOPE THAT THEY CAN GET THEIR PARENTS TO START MAKING THEM THAT WAY?

IN THE HOPE WE CAN THEN START TO COLLECT ROYALTIES FROM THEM.

CLICK

THE BEAUTY OF WHAT DAD DID IS SO BRILLIANT!...YET SO SIMPLE. BY PLACING THE JELLY BETWEEN TWO LAYERS OF PEANUT BUTTER, HE HAS MADE THE "SOGGY" PB&J VIRTUALLY OBSOLETE!

IF IT'S SO SIMPLE — HOW COME NO ONE'S THOUGHT OF IT BEFORE?

MAYBE SOMEONE HAS.

AND THAT'S WHERE I COME IN! WITHOUT A GOOD PUBLICIST LIKE ME, IT'S EASY FOR AN INDIVIDUAL'S ACCOMPLISHMENTS TO GO UNNOTICED.

BRIAN BASSET

FOR EXAMPLE: WHO INVENTED THE PEANUT BUTTER AND JELLY SANDWICH IN THE FIRST PLACE?

BEATS ME. NO PUBLICITY, I GUESS.

BINGO!

DING-DONG

ARE YOU CLAYTON'S DAD?

YES, I AM. HANG ON WHILE I GET HIM FOR YOU.

IT'S HIM! IT'S HIM!

BRIAN BASSET

NO, IT'S YOU WE WANT!.. AND ON BEHALF OF EVERY KID WHO NOW HAS HIS OR HER PEANUT BUTTER AND JELLY SANDWICH MADE THE ADAM NEWMAN WAY ..... THANK YOU, THANK YOU, THANK YOU!

LONG LIVE THE NON-SOGGY PB&J!

SAYYY, IF ONE OF YOU GROWS UP TO BECOME A TRAFFIC COP, PLEASE REMEMBER THIS IF YOU EVER HAVE TO PULL ME OVER.

UM.... YOU'RE WELCOME.

RING

HELLO, THIS IS ADAM.

BRIAN BASSET

HA-HA. VERY FUNNY.

LIKE I'M REALLY GOING TO FALL FOR ONE OF CLAYTON'S FRIENDS PRETENDING TO BE FROM THE "TODAY" SHOW WANTING ME ON THEIR SHOW TO TALK ABOUT THE "NEW" PB&J.

SLAM

I MUST ADMIT, THOUGH, THEY DID A PRETTY GOOD ADULT'S VOICE FOR A KID.

WAIT! MR. NEWMAN!! PLEASE, DON'T HANG UP! THIS REALLY IS THE NBC "TODAY" SHOW CALLING!

WE HEARD ABOUT HOW YOU'VE REINVENTED THE PEANUT BUTTER AND JELLY SANDWICH, AND WE'D LIKE TO HAVE YOU ON OUR SHOW TO TALK ABOUT IT.

BRIAN BASSET

UM... HOW DID YOU HEAR ABOUT ME?? I ONLY JUST STARTED PUTTING THE JELLY BETWEEN TWO LAYERS OF PEANUT BUTTER AS OF LAST WEEK!

NEWS OF THIS NATURE SPREADS QUICKLY.

LAURA! YOU'LL NEVER GUESS WHO ON OUR BLOCK IS GOING TO BE ON ONE OF THOSE NETWORK MORNING NEWS PROGRAMS THIS FRIDAY?!!

THAT NICE OLD MAN FROM DOWN THE STREET WHO HELPED SAVE ALL THOSE PEOPLE DURING WORLD WAR II?!

NO, ME! FOR REINVENTING THE PEANUT BUTTER AND JELLY SANDWICH!

BRIAN BASSET

I KNOW, KINDA PALES BY COMPARISON.

YOU THINK?

97

THANKS FOR DRIVING ME TO THE AIRPORT, LAURA.

KNOCK IT OFF. WE'RE ALL SO PROUD OF YOU, ADAM!

TO THINK— MY HUSBAND, THE MAN WHO REINVENTED THE PEANUT BUTTER AND JELLY SANDWICH.

MMM— HAVE A SAFE FLIGHT, AND WE'LL ALL BE WATCHING THE "TODAY" SHOW TOMORROW.

WOULDN'T THAT MAKE IT THE **TOMORROW SHOW** TOMORROW?

PLEASE PROMISE ME YOU WON'T TRY TO BE FUNNY ON THE SHOW.

OKAY, MR. NEWMAN, YOU'RE ON JUST AFTER THE MIDDLE EAST EXPERT.

UM... WHAT EXACTLY ARE YOU HERE TO BE INTERVIEWED ABOUT ANYWAY?

I REINVENTED THE PB&J BY PUTTING THE JELLY BETWEEN TWO LAYERS OF PEANUT BUTTER, THEREBY MAKING THE "SOGGY" PB&J A THING OF THE PAST.

GEEEZ— MY WIFE AND I HAVE BEEN FIXING OUR KIDS' SANDWICHES THAT WAY FOR YEARS.

OUR NEXT GUEST HAS JUST TAKEN THAT MUCH BELOVED ICON OF BAG LUNCHES EVERYWHERE TO NEW HEIGHTS. PLEASE WELCOME FROM... OH, MY GOSH, IT'S OUR VERY OWN...

I WONDER IF I STILL GET A "TODAY" SHOW COFFEE MUG?

REALLY, I'M PERFECTLY OKAY WITH NOT BEING THE ONE TO RECEIVE THE CREDIT FOR REINVENTING THE PEANUT BUTTER AND JELLY SANDWICH.

NOOO, IT'S MY KIDS I FEEL BAD FOR — ESPECIALLY MY OLDEST BOY. HE'S THE ONE WHO PUBLICIZED THE WHOLE THING.

I WOULDN'T WORRY ABOUT IT. KIDS ARE PRETTY RESILIENT.

CLAYTON, KATY! GET YOUR SHOES ON. I JUST CALLED THE AIRLINE AND YOUR FATHER'S FLIGHT IS ARRIVING 15 MINUTES EARLY.

(SIGH)
A BOOK DEAL WOULD'VE BOUGHT A HECK OF A LOT OF VIDEO GAMES.

BRIAN BASSET

HI. I'M CALLING ABOUT YOUR LATE PAYMENT.

BLESS THIS HOME OFFICE

NO, THIS ISN'T VISA OR MASTERCARD. THIS IS ADAM NEWMAN. I DO YOUR MONTHLY COMPANY NEWSLETTER.

NO, I DON'T TAKE VISA OR MASTERCARD.

BRIAN BASSET

HI, THIS IS ADAM NEWMAN. I DO YOUR COMPANY'S NEWSLETTER, AND...UM...I HAVEN'T RECEIVED A PAYMENT FOR QUITE A WHILE.

BLESS THIS HOME OFFICE

WHAT'S THAT YOU ASK?... AM I A SMALL OUTFIT OR A LARGE OUTFIT?

UM... LARGE.

...AND GETTING LARGER ALL THE TIME.... BUT WHAT DIFFERENCE DOES THAT MAKE??

BRIAN BASSET

BLESS THIS HOME OFFICE

CHIPS

I'M HOME. HOW'S IT GOING?

NOT GOOD.

BLESS THIS HOME OFFICE

Z

BRIAN BASSET

I SPENT MOST OF THE DAY CALLING EVERYONE WHO OWES MY BUSINESS MONEY.... AND TO NO AVAIL.

YOUR TROUBLE, ADAM, IS YOU'RE WAY TOO EASYGOING.

NOW WHAT I SUGGEST YOU... OH MY GOSH— LOOK AT THIS PLACE! I THOUGHT YOU'D AT LEAST HAVE THE KITCHEN CLEANED UP BY THE TIME I GOT HOME!??!

PERHAPS YOU COULD MAKE THESE CALLS FOR ME??

Adam @home
by Brian Basset

GRUNT!

WHOA! I TIED MY SHOES WITHOUT DOUBLE-GRUNTING.

LOOKING AWFULLY STUDLY, MR. NEWMAN! YOU'VE REALLY LOST SOME WEIGHT!

YOU'VE LOST WEIGHT, HAVEN'T YOU? YOU LOOK GREAT!

YOU LOOK TERRIFIC, ADAM! HAVE YOU LOST WEIGHT?!

? JUST EXACTLY HOW DID I LOOK BEFORE?

104

ADAM, YOU'RE AWFULLY QUIET TONIGHT.

YEAH, I KNOW... IT'S JUST THAT I WENT TO TRUMAN'S AFTER COFFEE TODAY AND SAW **HIS** HOME OFFICE.

NICE?!

NICE DOESN'T BEGIN TO DESCRIBE IT.

ADAM, TRUMAN'S A PSYCHOLOGIST WHO SEES PATIENTS FROM HIS HOME. YOUR CLIENTS, ON THE OTHER HAND, ARE ONLY VOICES ON THE PHONE.

FOR ALL THEY KNOW, YOUR OFFICE RIVALS THAT OF ANY MAJOR CEO!

UNTIL THE BUZZER ON THE DRYER GOES OFF.

SINCE WHEN DO YOU DO THE LAUNDRY THAT OFTEN??

BRIAN BASSET

I'M HOME.

I SMELL FRESH PAINT.

IT'S DAD. HE'S FIXING UP HIS OFFICE.

ADAM, PAINTING THE LAUNDRY ROOM ISN'T GOING TO MAKE IT APPEAR SIGNIFICANTLY...

...BIGGER.

HUH? DID YOU SAY SOMETHING?

BRIAN BASSET

OKAY, TEAM. WE HAVE A BIG GAME TOMORROW,

AND WHY IS IT IMPORTANT THAT EVERYONE GETS A GOOD NIGHT'S REST?

BRIAN BASSET

SO WE'LL BE ALERT ENOUGH TO REMEMBER WHAT FIELD TO GO TO.

UM, I WAS THINKING MORE ALONG THE LINE OF WHAT TO DO IF THE BALL IS HIT TO YOU.

OH-OH—AND TO REMEMBER WHO BRINGS THE TEAM SNACK.

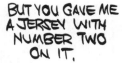

Panel 1: COACH, WHY DO YOU HAVE ME AT SECOND WHEN I THOUGHT I WAS PLAYING THIRD??

UM, NO. I'VE STILL GOT YOU AT THIRD.

Panel 2: BUT YOU GAVE ME A JERSEY WITH NUMBER TWO ON IT.

Panel 3: WEARING NUMBER TWO HAS NOTHING TO DO WITH SECOND BASE. ACTUALLY, SECOND BASE IS NUMBER FOUR IF YOU'RE KEEPING SCORE.

Panel 4: MAKE SENSE?

UM, SURE COACH.

HEY, TYLER! WANT TO TRADE YOUR NUMBER THREE FOR MY NUMBER TWO?!

WHY WOULD I WANT TO PLAY SECOND BASE?!

BRIAN BASSET

Panel 5: WHY DO YOU HAVE MY SON PLAYING THIRD BASE? HE'S A NATURAL SHORTSTOP.

Panel 6: BY MY CALCULATIONS, YOU'VE PLAYED THE OTHER KIDS AN AVERAGE OF 1/3 OF AN INNING MORE THAN MY SON.

BRIAN BASSET

Panel 7: MY SON HASN'T BATTED LEADOFF ALL SEASON! ...GRANTED, THEY'VE ONLY PLAYED TWO GAMES, BUT I SEE A PATTERN HERE.

Panel 8: Y'KNOW, YOUR NEGATIVE BODY LANGUAGE IS STARTING TO AFFECT THE PLAYERS. WHY DO YOU THINK THEY'RE A RUN DOWN RIGHT NOW?!

Panel 9: "TIME," UMP!

BRIAN BASSET

Panel 10:

Panel 11: WHOA! CLAYTON CALLED HIS "SHOT" JUST LIKE BABE RUTH.

Panel 12: YOU'RE RIGHT. THAT CLOUD DOES LOOK LIKE A 6-PIECE CHICKEN NUGGET.

TOLD YA.

COACH, I DON'T WANT TO BAT. PLEASE DON'T MAKE ME BAT.!

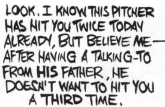

LOOK. I KNOW THIS PITCHER HAS HIT YOU TWICE TODAY ALREADY, BUT BELIEVE ME— AFTER HAVING A TALKING-TO FROM **HIS** FATHER, HE DOESN'T WANT TO HIT YOU A **THIRD** TIME.

BECAUSE THE BASES ARE LOADED?

NO, BECAUSE YOUR DAD'S A LAWYER.

BATTER UP!

LAURA, YOU'RE LATE FOR WORK.

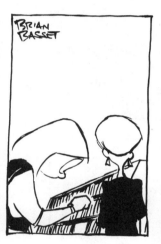

BRIAN BASSET

BY TWELVE SECONDS.

I HATE IT WHEN PEOPLE WITH ENGINEERING DEGREES GO INTO RETAIL.

GIGGLE GIGGLE Giggle Giggle Giggle Giggle Giggle

SEXUALITY

I DON'T KNOW WHAT THEY HAVE TO SNICKER ABOUT.

EVERY SURVEY OR ARTICLE I'VE READ SAYS TODAY'S TEENS ARE MORE THAN FAMILIAR WITH THE HUMAN BODY.

BRIAN BASSET

110

Adam @home

by Brian Basset

ARE YOU READY TO PAY FOR THAT?

YES, PLEASE!!

HERE, LET ME FIX THIS FOR YOU. THE JACKET'S BEEN TURNED UPSIDE DOWN.

THERE. MUCH BETTER.

YOU MEAN IT *ISN'T* A RARE MISPRINT???

SPLASH!

EXCUSE ME. COULD I SEE THAT WHEN YOU'RE DONE?

WOW. THESE COMPUTERS KEEP GETTING SMALLER AND SMALLER ALL THE TIME.

THAT'S A CALCULATOR.

RIGHT! IT COMPUTES NUMBERS, DOESN'T IT!?

HERE'S THE PLAYFUL SPERM WHALE HEADING BACK OUT TO OPEN WATERS.

DAD, WANNA TOSS THE BALL AROUND?

MAYBE LATER. RIGHT NOW I HAVE A CLIENT BREATHING DOWN MY NECK.

BRIAN BASSET

OKAY. I CAN TAKE A BREAK NOW.

SORRY. I DON'T TALK TO STRANGERS.

LOOK. I DON'T MEAN TO IGNORE YOU, AND IT'S NOT LIKE DADDY WANTS TO SIT IN FRONT OF A COMPUTER DURING THE DAY EITHER.

BUT YOU HAVE TO UNDERSTAND THAT **THIS** IS MY JOB. THIS IS HOW I HELP TO PUT SHOES ON YOUR FEET AND FOOD IN YOUR BELLY.

BRIAN BASSET

OKAY, WE CAN'T GO WITHOUT FOOD, BUT WE'LL GO BAREFOOT THE REST OF THE SUMMER IF YOU PLAY WITH US MORE.

OKAY... WHAT IF YOU HIRED US?

HIRED YOU??

YEAH. YOU'RE ALWAYS SAYING HOW PRODUCTIVE YOU'D BE IF WE DIDN'T BUG YOU SO MUCH, AND HOW YOU'D ACTUALLY HAVE MORE TIME FOR US IF YOU FINISHED YOUR WORK SOONER.

BRIAN BASSET

THAT'S NOT A BAD IDEA. LICKING ENVELOPES AND STAMPS WOULD SAVE ME SOME TIME...

A JOB?!? NO, WE MEAN PAY US NOT TO BOTHER YOU.

Ad@m

by Brian Basset

SCREEECH

ADAM, WHY ARE WE STOPPING HALF A BLOCK FROM HOME??

DO YOU HAVE ANY MONEY FOR THE BABY SITTER?? I KNOW I DON'T.

NONE, I LEFT IT ALL FOR THE TIP.

OKAY, UM... CHECK UNDER THE SEATS AND BETWEEN THE CUSHIONS, THERE'S GOTTA BE SOMETHING.

BRIAN BASSET

HERE'S A DIME. ...AND A PENNY.

...OOW, OOW, A QUARTER!!

I FOUND A FRENCH FRY.

67 CENTS AND A FRENCH FRY??

A PETRIFIED FRENCH FRY! IT COULD BE WORTH MILLIONS!

WE'LL WRITE YOU A CHECK.

KATY! CLAYTON! INTERESTED IN GOING CAMPING NEXT WEEK?

WOULD WE GET TO SIT AROUND A CAMPFIRE AND ROAST MARSHMALLOWS?!!

AND HAVE A CONTEST TO SEE WHO HAS THE MOST MOSQUITO BITES LIKE LAST TIME?!

LET'S NOT FORGET WHO WON FOR HAVING THE **LARGEST** MOSQUITO BITE!

YOU CHEATED! **THAT** WAS REALLY POISON IVY!!

SURE! SOUNDS LIKE FUN.

BRIAN BASSET

BRIAN BASSET

WELL, TROOPS — THIS IS IT, OUR HOME FOR THE NEXT FOUR DAYS. CAMPSITE 39B.

THE GROUND'S KINDA ROCKY.

C'MON. LET'S PITCH THE TENT BEFORE IT GETS DARK.

BRIAN BASSET

OOPS.

ADAM, MAYBE THERE'S A REASON EARLY HUMANS LEFT THEIR CAVES, EVOLVED, AND BUILT RESORT HOTELS.

OKAY. I'VE PICKED OUT MY SIDE OF THE TENT.

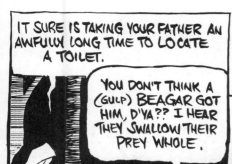

IT SURE IS TAKING YOUR FATHER AN AWFULLY LONG TIME TO LOCATE A TOILET.

YOU DON'T THINK A (GULP) BEAGAR GOT HIM, D'YA?? I HEAR THEY SWALLOW THEIR PREY WHOLE.

NOOOOO, AND WHAT IN THE WORLD IS A BEAGAR??

IT'S A CREATURE THAT'S HALF BEAR, HALF COUGAR.

BUT IF IT ATE DAD WHOLE, WOULDN'T THAT MAKE IT ⅓ DAD, ⅓ BEAR AND ⅓ COUGAR?

OH MY GOSH... THE DREADED DADBEAGAR!

BRIAN BASSET

DANG. NO TOILET PAPER! ...AND I TOLD THE KIDS I'D ROAST MARSHMALLOWS WITH THEM NEARLY 30 MINUTES AGO.

IF NO ONE COMES WITH TOILET PAPER SOON, I MAY JUST HAVE TO MAKE A RUN FOR IT.

BRIAN BASSET

SHOULDN'T YOU GO LOOK FOR DAD??

AND LEAVE YOU HERE ALL ALONE?!?

DON'T WORRY. IF ANY STRANGE CREATURE STUMBLES OUT OF THE DARK, WE'LL FLING RED-HOT MARSHMALLOWS AT ITS BUTT.

MA'AM, I'M SURE YOUR HUSBAND IS JUST FINE. THIS SORT OF THING HAPPENS MORE THAN YOU THINK.

HUSBANDS DISAPPEARING INTO THE PITCH-DARK WHILE TRYING TO FIND THE TOILET??

SURE! ACTUALLY, LESS IN THE WINTER MONTHS. HE PROBABLY SAW THE WARM, GENTLE CAMP FIRE COMING FROM THE NUDIST COLONY ACROSS THE LAKE. I'LL BE HAPPY TO CHECK IT OUT.

THIS IS RIDICULOUS! SOMEBODY'S GOTTA SHOW UP WITH TOILET PAPER!....OH MY GOSH.... MY BUTT'S ASLEEP. I CAN'T FEEL MY BUTT!

IS ANYONE IN THERE?

YES! YES! DO YOU HAVE ANY TOILET PAPER?!

UM... JUST A SECOND.

FINALLY! THANK GOODNESS.

WAIT'LL LAURA HEARS ABOUT MY PREDICAMENT.

BRIAN BASSET

HE'S OKAY!!

I HATE COMING BACK TO WORK AFTER A VACATION.

CLICK

YOU HAVE 300 E-MAILS.

HECK, THEY DON'T KNOW I'M NOT STILL ON VACATION!

BRIAN BASSET

SEEMS SLOWER THAN USUAL.

TAKE YOUR BREAK EARLY THEN.

SA 10% 40% EVE

BRIAN BASSET

SERIOUS??

SURE! NO NEED FOR BOTH OF US UP HERE.

THANKS!

NO....

.....PROBLEM.

MMMMM, THAT'S THE SPOT.

CAN YOU FEEL HOW TIGHT AND TENSE IT IS?

NOT REALLY. IT FEELS SOFT TO ME.

I DIDN'T SAY YOU HAD A "FAT" NECK!!

TENNIS CAMP???

YEAH. BASKETBALL CAMP WAS ALL FULL. GET YOUR TENNIS SHOES ON.

I DON'T HAVE TENNIS SHOES. I HAVE BASKETBALL SHOES FOR BASKETBALL!! I DON'T WANNA PLAY TENNIS!

WELL, WHEN I WAS A KID, ALL GYM SHOES WERE CALLED TENNIS SHOES.

THAT DOESN'T MAKE SENSE.

JUST GET YOUR 'AIR-SAMPRAS' ON.

HELLO, CAMPERS! MY NAME IS RYAN, AND I'LL BE YOUR TENNIS COACH.

I SEE A HAND IN THE BACK. YES?

DID YOU EVER WIN WIMBLEDON OR THE U.S. OPEN?

HA-HA. FUNNY. OKAY, TROOPS, IF EVERYONE WILL PLEASE FOLLOW ME TO THE NEXT COURT...

(AHEM) I'M WAITING.

LISTEN TO ME, EVERYBODY. I'LL BET HE DOESN'T HAVE A DECENT SHOE ENDORSEMENT EITHER.

WHERE ARE YOUR OTHER TWO CHILDREN, MR. NEWMAN — YOU DIDN'T WANT TO BRING THEM IN?

OH HI, ANGIE. NO— THEY'RE AT TENNIS CAMP.

BRIAN BASSET

HOW FUN!

WE'LL SEE.

MY OLDEST ISN'T TOO WILD ABOUT THE IDEA.

CLAYTON! GET DOWN NOW!

I'M GOING OVER THE WALL! NO ONE CAN STOP ME!!

UM... CAN YOU GIVE ME A BOOST?

BRIAN BASSET

OKAY, CLAYTON, LISTEN UP. I'M GOING TO ROCKET A SERVE RIGHT AT YOUR NOGGIN. WHAT SHOULD YOU DO?

FLING MY RACKET AT YOU!

CLAYTON, YOU PLAY **UP** WHILE YOUR SISTER PLAYS **BACK**. THIS IS CALLED "MIXED DOUBLES."

BRIAN BASSET

NO WAY! I WANT TO PLAY "BACK"!

AND WHY IS THAT?

SO I CAN NAIL HER IN THE BACK WITH A SHOT!

CLASS, MY NAME IS AMY, AND I'LL BE YOUR NEW TENNIS INSTRUCTOR FOR THE REMAINDER OF CAMP.

WHAT HAPPENED TO RYAN?!

APPARENTLY, TEACHING KIDS TENNIS WAS SOMETHING HE WASN'T QUITE READY FOR.

DID HE GO INTO ANOTHER SPORT?

NO, THE PRIESTHOOD.

APPARENTLY, KIDS WERE SOMETHING HE WASN'T QUITE READY FOR EITHER. LOOK, I'M UPSET, TOO — HE WAS MY FIANCE!

MY PARENTS GOT A PUPPY BEFORE THEY HAD ME.

YOU DON'T THINK MY PRETENDING TO CHOKE ON A TENNIS BALL WAS TOO MUCH FOR HIM, D'YA ??

WHICH TIME?

ON THE **BACKHAND** YOU WANT TO TAKE YOUR RACKET ALL THE WAY BACK IN ONE MOTION AND...

MMMPHM MPHPPPM MMPHHM

YES, WHAT IS IT NOW, CLAYTON?

HE SAYS HE CAN BALANCE HIS TENNIS RACKET BY STICKING HIS TONGUE BETWEEN THE STRINGS.

MMMPHMMP MMMMMPHH MPHHMMM MHPMMM

YOU WERE RIGHT, COACH. WITH PRACTICE COMES SUCCESS!

LEMME TRY!

NICE SHOT, CLAYTON. OKAY, NOW **CHARGE** THE NET!

WHACK!

Y'KNOW— RUN UP ON IT.

THAT'S IT!

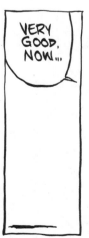

VERY GOOD, NOW...

BRIAN BASSET

SPROING!

COOL!

WE'LL MEET UP WITH YOU AND CLAYTON BY THE CINNAMON ROLL PLACE ON THE SECOND LEVEL IN TWO HOURS, OKAY?

WHAT?? THAT DOESN'T GIVE YOU ENOUGH TIME TO SHOP FOR SCHOOL CLOTHES??

I GUESS IT DOES.

IT'S JUST THAT THERE ARE FOUR ESPRESSO PLACES AT EITHER END OF THE MALL I'D LIKE TO DROP IN ON.

WOULDN'T THAT SPEED UP YOUR SHOPPING??

FINE, WE'LL MEET YOU IN FRONT OF THE CINNAMON ROLL PLACE IN TWO HOURS.

HUH?? WHO IS THIS??

DAD, THIS IS ERIK. HE'S GOING TO BE MY FASHION CONSULTANT.

I RENTED HIM.

YOU RENTED HIM??

SURE. LOTS OF TEENAGERS WILL WORK IF IT'S NOT REALLY "WORK."

I'M HUNGRY. YOU SAID YOUR DAD WOULD TAKE ME TO THE FOOD COURT.

HOW MUCH?

$54.95

THAT'S NOT SO BAD.

THAT'S JUST FOR THE LACES.

BRIAN BASSET

THE
END